THE UNIVERSE

Comets, Asteroids, and Meteors

Revised and Updated

Dr. Raman K. Prinja

Heinemann Library
Chicago, Illinois

Customer Service 888-454-2279
Visit our website at www.heinemannraintree.com

Designed by Richard Parker and Manhattan Design
Illustrations by Art Construction
Printed in China by Leo Paper Group

12 11 10 09 08
10 9 8 7 6 5 4 3 2 1

New edition ISBNs: 9781432901622 (hardcover)
                   9781432901745 (paperback)

The Library of Congress has cataloged the first edition as follows:
Prinja, Raman, 1961 -
Comets, asteroids, and meteors / Raman Prinja
v. cm. -- (The universe)
Includes bibliographical references and index.
ISBN 1-58810-909-7 (hardcover) -- ISBN 1-40340-610-3 (pbk.)
1. Comets--Juvenile literature. 2. Asteroids--Juvenile literature.
3. Meteors--Juvenile literature. [1. Comets. 2. Meteors. 3. Asteroids] I. Title. II. Series.
QB721.5 .P75 2002
523.6--dc21
                              2002004058

Acknowledgments
The publishers would like to thank the following for permission to reproduce photographs: AKG London p. 11; Galaxy Picture Library p. 27; John Hopkins University (Applied Physics Laboratory) p. 21; NASA pp. 6, 25; Science Photo Library pp. 4, 5, 7, 8, 10, 12, 13, 14, 15, 16, 17, 19, 20, 22, 23, 24, 26, 28, 29.

Cover photograph reproduced with permission of Science Photo Library/Mark Garlick.

The publishers would like to thank Geza Gyuk of the Adler Planetarium, Chicago, for his assistance in the preparation of this book.

Every effort has been made to contact copyright holders of any material reproduced in this book. Any omissions will be rectified in subsequent printings if notice is given to the publishers.

Contents

Any words appearing in the text in bold, **like this**, are explained in the glossary.

What Are Comets, Asteroids, and Meteors?

The Sun, the **planets,** and their moons are not the only members of our **solar system**. There are also billions of other lumps of ice and rock called comets and asteroids. Meteors are pieces of rock or dust that travel in outer space. These objects were left over from when the solar system formed about 4.5 billion years ago.

This stunning picture shows Comet Hyakutake, which blazed across our skies in March 1996.

This is a close-up view of the head and tail of Comet Hyakutake.

Comets

Comets are like dirty snowballs made of ice, dust, and gases. They travel around the Sun in long, oval-shaped **orbits**. As they get closer to the Sun, the ice melts and a gigantic tail of gas and dust forms.

Comets are rarely seen in the sky. Amazing comets with beautiful, long tails appear about once every 10 to 15 years. More often, they do not look like much more than faint, fuzzy "stars." Although comets travel very fast in space, because they are so far away, they seem to move slowly across the sky over several nights.

Asteroids

Asteroids are lumps of rock drifting in space. They vary in size from 3 feet (1 meter) across to being nearly one-third the size of Earth's Moon. There are many billions of asteroids moving around the Sun between the **orbits** of Mars and Jupiter.

Only a couple of asteroids are bright enough for us to see them in the sky with our naked eyes. Even with a good pair of binoculars or a **telescope**, they are hard to spot and only look like specks of light.

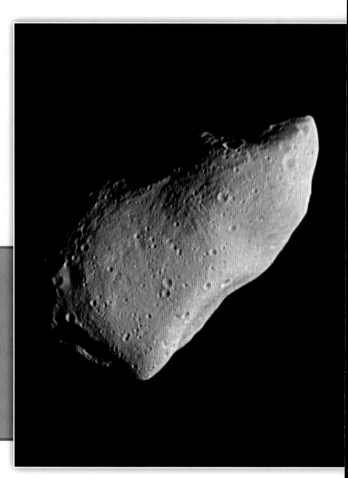

This picture of an asteroid called Gaspra was taken by the *Galileo* **spacecraft** when it was only 3,300 miles (5,300 kilometers) away from its surface.

Meteors

Sometimes bits of dust or rocks from space come so close to Earth that **gravity** pulls them into its **atmosphere**. They then tear through Earth's atmosphere and produce a lot of heat. The lights we see are made by the incredibly hot pieces of rock burning. These fiery objects are called meteors.

This picture shows how beautiful meteors are in the night sky.

Meteors look like fast-moving streaks of light in the sky at night. That is why they are sometimes called "shooting stars" or "falling stars." They flash across the sky in just a few seconds and can appear in any part of the sky at any time. Meteor streaks are common, and you can usually see a few every hour. Most look white, but red, yellow, or even green meteor streaks have also been spotted.

Why are they called comets, asteroids, and meteors?

The word *comet* comes from comets' flowing tails and from the ancient Greek word *kometes*, meaning "long-haired."

The ancient Greek word *asteroid* means "like a star."

The word *meteor* comes from the Greek word *meteoron*, which means "a special event in the sky."

During some days of the year, many more meteors than usual can be seen. This is a **meteor shower**.

Where Do Comets Come From?

Most of the comets we see in the sky start their journeys from a very distant region of space called the **Oort cloud**. The Oort cloud is in the furthest part of our **solar system**, further out than the **orbit** of Pluto. It is between 2 trillion and 10 trillion miles (3 trillion and 15 trillion kilometers) away, thousands of times further away than the Sun and almost halfway to the next closest star.

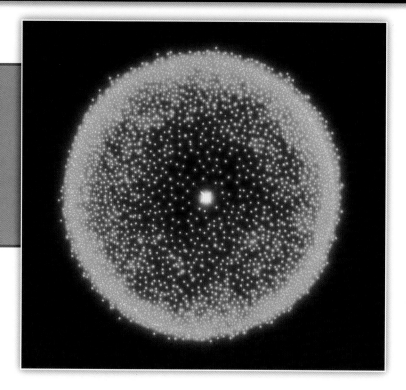

The Oort cloud is home to a huge swarm of comets, which surround the planets in the solar system.

There are many billions of comets in the Oort cloud, but they are all very cold, dead lumps of ice, dust, and rock. Most of them are only a few miles across. There are also billions more comets that orbit the Sun, between Neptune and the Oort cloud. This second collection of comets is called the **Kuiper belt**. Some scientists think Pluto is just the brightest object in the Kuiper belt.

Some fall toward the Sun

While they are in the Oort cloud and Kuiper belt, the comets are frozen, dark objects that we cannot see. They do not glow or have flowing tails. Sometimes, however, a comet can get knocked out of these regions, perhaps by crashing into another comet. The comet's path is then changed, flinging it toward the inner part of the solar system because of the pull of the Sun's **gravity**. It then starts to orbit the Sun.

Their new orbits around the Sun are not circles like those of most of the **planets**, but rather long, oval shapes. These comets can take hundreds or even thousands of years to finish one lap around the Sun.

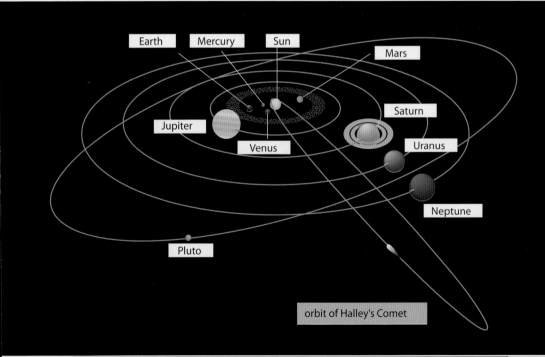

Earth Mercury Sun Mars Saturn Jupiter Venus Uranus Neptune Pluto orbit of Halley's Comet

The comets seen in the sky move around the Sun in very stretched, oval orbits.

Why Do Comets Have Tails?

As a comet gets closer to the Sun, it begins to warm up. What started as a dark, frozen object turns into one so bright that we can see it from Earth. This change happens because the heat from the Sun burns off the ice on the comet's surface. The heated gases start to glow and the comet starts to squirt huge fountains of gas and dust into space. As the comet nears the Sun, the jets of gas and dust make enormous tails of material that stretch for millions of miles. The comet can lose over 50 tons of gas and dust every second! It may now appear as a bright sight in our skies.

Comets have two types of tail. They have a **dust tail** made of **microscopic** grains of dust. A dust tail is not straight, but rather slightly curved. Comets also have a blue **gas tail** made of hot gas, which is straighter and narrower.

The tail of a comet always points away from the Sun. This is because it is being pushed back by a flow of electric **particles** blowing off the Sun. This flow is called the **solar wind**. The solar wind acts like a fan that blows the comet's tail away from the Sun.

Comet West was seen in the skies during March 1976. It has a narrow, blue gas tail and a wide, white dust tail.

The show must end

After many months, a comet will move around the Sun and head back into the outermost regions of the **solar system**. As it glides away from the heat of the Sun, the comet's surface cools down and starts to freeze over again. It returns to being a dark object, lost deep in space and no longer seen from Earth. It may be hundreds or thousands of years before that same comet returns to our part of the solar system and heats up again.

Comets were not always liked

Comets in the sky have caused fear and panic through the ages. For thousands of years people thought comets brought bad news. This is because, unlike the Sun, Moon, and stars, comets came and went without warning.

Comets have been blamed for many things on Earth. In 79 CE, a comet appeared in the sky during the eruption of Mount Vesuvius, a volcano that destroyed the Roman city of Pompeii.

Some people, however, thought that comets were a good sign. After the death of the Roman leader Julius Caesar, many people were happy, and so they celebrated a comet that appeared in Europe in 44 BCE.

The famous Bayeaux Tapestry shows Halley's Comet (upper right) in 1066.

What Is a Comet Made Of?

Apart from its tail, a comet is made of two other main parts called a **nucleus** and a **coma**.

Fragile nucleus

The solid part at the center of a comet is called the nucleus. It may only be a few miles across. Unlike the **planets**, which are the shape of balls, it is an odd shape. The nucleus of a comet is made of loose dust and rock that is held together by ice. The ice is not only frozen water, but also frozen gases such as **carbon dioxide**.

A comet's coma

When the comet approaches the Sun, the ice in the nucleus starts to melt and gases begin to escape. This is when the nucleus becomes surrounded by a cloud of material called a coma. The bright coma can measure more than 60,000 miles (100,000 kilometers) across. That is nearly the size of the giant planet Saturn. The coma and the nucleus together make up the head of the comet.

This is the nucleus of Halley's Comet, as seen by the *Giotto* spacecraft in 1986.

This is computer-generated artwork of the spacecraft *Stardust*, which passed through the gas and dust cloud of Comet Wild on January 2, 2004. *Stardust* passed by the comet at a speed of 4 miles (6 kilometers) per second!

How close have we gotten to a comet?

A few **spacecraft** have been sent from Earth to fly very close to comets. One of these was the *Giotto* spacecraft, which flew to within 370 miles (600 kilometers) of Halley's Comet in 1986. *Giotto* discovered the comet had a potato-shaped nucleus that was 9.3 miles (15 kilometers) long and 5 miles (8 kilometers) wide. There were hills and valleys on the surface of the comet, with powerful jets of gas blowing out to make a tail.

Another spacecraft, called *Stardust*, was launched in 1999 toward Comet Wild. It flew by the comet in 2004, collecting **particles** of dust and photographing the nucleus. In 2006 *Stardust* returned samples of the dust to Earth. The material is being studied by scientists across the world and is teaching us new things about how the **solar system** formed.

Which Are the Most Famous Comets?

Thousands of comets have been discovered, but only a few of them are well known to us today, because they are exciting to watch. The most famous comets are Halley's Comet, Comet Hale-Bopp, and Comet Kohoutek.

Halley's Comet

The most famous comet in history is Halley's Comet. It is named after the British **astronomer** Edmond Halley, who first figured out the comet's **orbit** in 1705. Although most comets are named after the people who first find them, Halley did not actually discover this comet. Chinese astronomers had seen it over 2,000 years ago.

Halley's Comet passes through our skies every 76 years. It last appeared in 1986 and will return in the year 2062. Along its orbit in 1986, the comet came within 50 million miles (80 million kilometers) of the Sun and passed 40 million miles (65 million kilometers) away from Earth.

Sir Edmond Halley (1656–1742) was a famous British astronomer.

Comet Hale-Bopp

Comet Hale-Bopp was a magnificent sight in the night skies during 1997. At the head of the comet was a very bright **coma**, which was followed by two magnificent, sweeping tails.

Comet Hale-Bopp passed by about 122 million miles (197 million kilometers) away from Earth, which is nearly one and a half times the distance between Earth and the Sun. The comet was moving at a speed of 1.2 million miles (2 million kilometers) per day. Sadly, Comet Hale-Bopp takes so long to complete an orbit around the Sun that it will not be back in our skies for another 3,600 years!

Comet Kohoutek

Comet Kohoutek was discovered in March 1973 by an astronomer named Lubos Kohoutek. He found it by accident, when it was still a long way from the Sun. There was a lot of excitement because people thought that when the comet got closer to the Sun and heated up, it would become the most amazing comet seen for 100 years.

Although it had a beautiful tail, Comet Kohoutek stayed dim and never lived up to all the excitement. It will not return to our skies for another 75,000 years.

Do Comets Ever Crash?

The surfaces of Earth's Moon and the **planet** Mercury have a very large number of **craters** on them. These are bowl-shaped holes that were made billions of years ago when comets or asteroids crashed there.

If it were not for the wearing away, or **erosion**, of land by rain and wind, Earth's surface would also have lots of scars from crashed comets and asteroids. A few scars do still remain today. A 2,600-feet- (800-meter-) wide crater left by a crash 50,000 years ago can still be seen in Arizona. Besides hitting planets and moons, some comets pass so close to the Sun that they boil away in the heat and light and disappear forever.

A crash into Jupiter

In March 1993 **astronomers** discovered a comet called Shoemaker-Levy 9, which had broken into more than 20 small pieces, each about 0.6 miles (1 kilometer) across. The pieces of the comet passed so close to Jupiter that the giant planet's strong **gravity** pulled them in.

The Barringer Crater in Arizona is about 650 feet (200 meters) deep and 2,600 feet (800 meters) wide. It was made when a huge rock crashed into Earth.

The broken-up comet finally crashed into Jupiter between July 16 and July 22, 1994. The lumps of rock and ice thumped into Jupiter's **atmosphere** and exploded in huge fireballs. They left large, dark blotches made of gas and dust in the upper layers of Jupiter's atmosphere. These scars were the size of Earth and could be seen on the surface of Jupiter for more than a year.

Dark, Earth-sized patches were seen in the atmosphere of Jupiter after pieces of a comet crashed there.

What killed the dinosaurs?

One of the great mysteries about the dinosaurs is why they died out so suddenly. Most scientists think that the dinosaurs died when a large comet or asteroid slammed into Earth about 65 million years ago. The object was about 6 miles (10 kilometers) wide and was traveling a hundred times faster than a bullet when it crashed close to Mexico, in Central America.

There was a huge explosion due to the crash, and it sent massive amounts of dust up into the atmosphere. The dust blocked out the light of the Sun for many months. Earth got cooler, the rains became poisonous, there were lots of fires, and the plants died. The dinosaurs became **extinct** around this time because they could not survive all these changes to the planet.

What Are Asteroids and Where Do They Come From?

Asteroids are lumps of rock that were left over after the Sun and **planets** were made about 4.5 billion years ago. There are only around 200 asteroids larger than 60 miles (100 kilometers), but many millions of smaller ones. Although asteroids are mainly made of rocks, dust, and water ice, they also contain metals such as iron and nickel.

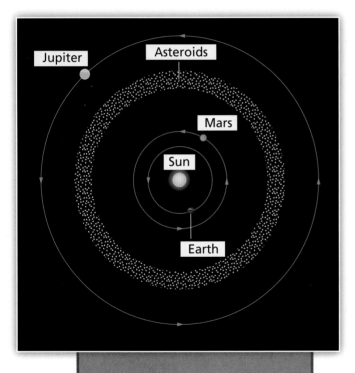

Most of the asteroids in our solar system are in a belt between the orbits of Mars and Jupiter.

The main belt

Most of these ancient rocks are found **orbiting** the Sun between the planets Mars and Jupiter. This region is called the **Asteroid Belt** and is the home of millions of asteroids, most smaller than half a mile across. The largest asteroid in this belt is Ceres. It is 590 miles (950 kilometers) across, which is almost a quarter of the size of Earth's Moon. Ceres is so large that **astronomers** sometimes consider it a "dwarf planet."

Jupiter is the largest planet in the **solar system**. Astronomers think that the strong pull of its **gravity** stopped the asteroids from gathering together to form another planet where the Asteroid Belt is now.

Getting really close to asteroids

Most asteroids are too small and faint for us to learn much about them from Earth, even with very large **telescopes**. Over the past few years, we have discovered more about asteroids by sending **spacecraft** to visit them.

While on its journey to the giant planet Jupiter, a spacecraft called *Galileo* gave us our first close-up view of an asteroid. Between 1991 and 1993 it flew past the rocky objects called Gaspra and Ida. In 1997 the *NEAR* (Near Earth Asteroid Rendezvous) *Shoemaker* spacecraft passed close by an odd-shaped boulder called Mathilde. *Shoemaker* then went on to become the first spacecraft to ever go into orbit around an asteroid, when it circled Eros in 2000. A year later it actually landed on Eros, but it stopped working soon after.

The *Galileo* spacecraft took this picture of asteroid Ida and its tiny moon, Dactyl.

This is an artist's idea of the *NEAR* (Near Earth Asteroid Rendezvous) spacecraft **orbiting** the asteroid Eros.

Piles of rubble

The excellent pictures sent back by **spacecraft** like *Galileo* and *NEAR* showed us that asteroids are rocky objects with lots of **craters** on their surface. Amazingly, they also found that many asteroids are not solid, but rather seem to be made of several pieces. They are more like loosely glued piles of rubble and pebbles.

Another surprise was that the craters on some asteroids are very large. Mathilde is only 40 miles (66 kilometers) long, but it has a crater that is almost 18 miles (30 kilometers) wide and 3.7 miles (6 kilometers) deep. A smaller asteroid crashing into Mathilde caused this crater.

This was one of the last pictures sent by the *NEAR* spacecraft. It shows an area of 40 feet (12 meters) across. Some of the larger rocks are just a little smaller than a person!

Could I visit an asteroid?

You could land on an asteroid, but there would be no air to breathe and no water to drink. The surface would be hilly, with lots of craters and ditches. It would take you less than an hour to walk all around a typical asteroid in the **Asteroid Belt**. Since most asteroids are so small, their **gravity** is very weak. This means you would feel very lightweight standing on the surface. A normal adult would weigh as little as a couple of spoonfuls of sugar on Eros. Some scientists have suggested that after returning to the Moon, National Aeronautics and Space Administration (NASA) should send an astronaut to an asteroid.

Why Do We Need to Study Asteroids?

Most asteroids are safely tucked away in the **Asteroid Belt** between Mars and Jupiter. However, some have strayed out of this region and have ended up much closer to Earth. Scientists need to study these stray asteroids because there is a chance that one might smash into our **planet**.

An area of thick forest almost 25 miles (40 kilometers) across in Siberia, Russia, was destroyed in 1908 when an asteroid exploded there. Luckily, no one was killed.

A huge area of forest was destroyed in Russia when an asteroid exploded there in 1908.

If an asteroid the size of a football stadium smashed into one of Earth's oceans, it would make huge waves that could destroy cities along the coasts. A crash from a 6-mile- (10-kilometer-) wide asteroid or comet would be a threat to almost all life on our planet.

This is an artist's idea of a giant asteroid smashing into Earth. If this impact happened today, it could destroy all life on our planet.

No need to panic

There is no need to panic. The chances of an asteroid actually hitting Earth are very small. No asteroid or comet is known to be heading toward us today, but we do need to stay on the lookout. There are more than 100,000 asteroids, each the size of a football stadium, that could pass close to Earth. All around the world **astronomers** use **telescopes** to watch these asteroids. This way they can figure out if any of them might be a danger to us.

What could be done?

In the very unlikely event that scientists discover an asteroid in space heading toward Earth, we will hopefully know about it many years before it gets close. There would then be enough time to launch rockets to the asteroid and set off huge explosions above its surface. The force of the explosions would change the asteroid's **orbit** slightly, causing it to miss Earth and thus keep us safe.

What Is the Difference Between Meteors and Meteorites?

The **solar system** is littered with lots of small rocks and bits of dust. Some are called meteors and some are called **meteorites**. As Earth moves in its **orbit** around the Sun, only meteorites will strike the **planet**. They heat up by rubbing against the planet's **atmosphere**. This is called **friction**, and it works in the same way that you can warm up your hands by rubbing them against each other.

Some scientists think that this meteorite, found in Antarctica in 1984, was blasted from the surface of Mars about 3.5 billion years ago.

The smaller objects from space heat up and burn completely in the atmosphere. They leave behind flashing lights in the sky called meteors. Anything between the size of dust grains to a few inches across will be too small to survive the journey through the atmosphere to Earth's surface. They will completely burn up as meteors.

Chunks that land

Some chunks of material approaching our planet from space are large enough to survive the scorching trip through Earth's atmosphere. Pieces that land on our planet's surface are called meteorites. They are usually just a few inches across when they land.

Three or four meteorites hit Earth every day. Luckily, very few people have ever been struck or hurt by a meteorite.

These scientists are collecting meteorites on the icy surface of Antarctica.

Finding meteorites is important because they are very old objects. This means that scientists can use them to learn more about the solar system when it was first made, billions of years ago. Most meteorites are pieces of broken-up comets or asteroids. Amazingly, some have even been blasted from Mars or the Moon and have crashed on to Earth. Antarctica, near Earth's **South Pole**, is a good place for finding meteorites. They are dark and easy to spot against the bright, white ice.

Most meteorites are made of stone or rock. A few are made of metals like iron, and a tiny number are a mixture of stone and iron.

What Are Meteor Showers?

If you look at a dark, starry sky, you will sometimes see streaks or flashes of light. These are meteors, and you can usually see two or three of them every hour, every night. During some months of the year, many more meteors than normal can be seen at night. Perhaps as many as 100 meteors per hour may streak across the skies, looking like fireworks displays. These "displays" are called **meteor showers**.

One of the greatest meteor showers ever seen was on November 12, 1833. People living in Europe and the United States saw almost 100 meteors every second!

Comet dust

Comets that pass close to Earth leave behind huge clouds of tiny dust grains. The material is spread in space, all through the **orbit** of the comet.

This Perseid meteor trail was photographed in Finland. The Perseids are meteors that are usually seen around August 12 each year.

Meteor showers happen when Earth passes through these clouds of leftover comet dust. At this time, lots of dust grains crash into Earth's **atmosphere** and burn up as bright streaks of light.

The meteor shower ends when Earth has completely passed through the dust cloud. We then have to wait a few months for the next meteor shower, when Earth comes across the dust of another comet.

Showers to look out for

Most meteor showers seem to start from single points in the sky and streak out like exploding fireworks. The showers are named after the **constellation** of stars from which they seem to spread out. The displays are much easier to see in dark areas, away from city lights.

The best meteor showers that you can look out for every year in the **northern hemisphere** are the Quadrantis shower on January 1–5, the Perseids shower on August 10–15, the Leonids shower on November 14–20, and the Geminids shower on December 10–19. The Perseids, Leonids, and Geminids showers can also be seen every year from Australia and other countries in the **southern hemisphere**.

A Leonids meteor shower is seen here in 1999.

Fact File

Here are some interesting facts about comets, asteroids, and meteors:

- The **Oort cloud**, where most comets come from, stretches from around 2 trillion to 10 trillion miles (3 trillion to 15 trillion kilometers) away. The *New Horizons* **spacecraft**, which will take nine years to reach Pluto, will take more than 5,000 years to reach the inner edge of the Oort cloud!

- The dust grains that were caused during the Perseids **meteor shower** every August were left behind by a comet that passed close to Earth in 1862. The dust grains that were caused during the Leonids meteor shower every November were left behind by a comet called Tempel-Tuttle.

- The **Asteroid Belt**, where most of the asteroids are found, is about three times farther away from the Sun than Earth.

- There are probably over one million asteroids larger than about half a mile (1 kilometer) across. Even though there are so many, most are so small that all of the asteroids together would still be much less massive than the Moon.

A bright, glowing comet can be one of the most amazing sights of nature.

This is an artist's idea of the *Rosetta* Lander probe on the surface of Comet Churyumov-Gerasimenko.

- Comets move through space at speeds of many miles per second.

- Meteors enter Earth's **atmosphere** at speeds of around 60,000 miles (100,000 kilometers) per hour. After being slowed down by the atmosphere, a small **meteorite** will be moving at only a few hundred miles per hour when it strikes the ground.

- In 2004 the European Space Agency (ESA) launched the *Rosetta* spacecraft toward a comet called Churyumov-Gerasimenko. It will land on the comet in 2014 to study its surface.

Numbers
One thousand is written as 1,000. One million is 1,000,000 and one billion is 1,000,000,000.

Glossary

Asteroid Belt doughnut-shaped collection of asteroids found between the orbits of Mars and Jupiter

astronomer scientist who studies objects in space, such as planets and stars

atmosphere layers of gases that surround a planet

carbon dioxide gas contained in Earth's atmosphere

coma large blob of gas that surrounds the nucleus of a comet as it gets close to the Sun

constellation imaginary pattern or picture formed in the sky by a group of stars

crater bowl-shaped hole made on the surface of a planet or moon by a rocky object crashing from space

dust tail part of a comet's tail made up of tiny dust grains

erosion wearing away

extinct no longer living, such as an animal species that has died out

friction force between two objects when they rub against each other

gas tail part of a comet's tail that is made up of gas

gravity force that pulls all objects toward the surface of Earth or any other planet, moon, or star

Kuiper belt region beyond Neptune that scientists think contains large numbers of comets

meteorite bit of material that enters Earth from space and falls to the ground

meteor shower event during certain times of the year when many meteors can be seen every hour

microscopic something extremely tiny that can only be seen using a microscope

northern hemisphere half of Earth between the North Pole and the equator

nucleus center of an object, such as a comet

Oort cloud huge group of rocks and dust that surround the solar system. This is the home of most comets.

orbit path taken by an object as it moves around another body (planet or star). The Moon follows an orbit around Earth.

particle very small piece, or amount, of an object or material

planet large object (for example, Earth) moving around a star (for example, the Sun)

solar system group of eight planets and other objects orbiting the Sun

solar wind steady stream of material given off by the Sun

southern hemisphere half of Earth between the South Pole and the equator

South Pole point due south that marks the end of an imaginary line, called an axis, about which a planet spins

spacecraft vehicle that travels beyond Earth and into space

telescope instrument used by astronomers to study objects in outer space

More Books to Read

Cole, Michael D. *Comets and Asteroids: Ice and Rocks in Space.* Berkeley Heights, N.J.: Enslow, 2003.

Koppes, Steven N. *Killer Rocks from Outer Space: Asteroids, Comets, and Meteors.* Minneapolis: Lerner, 2004.

Index